Would You Rather...
Dine with a DUNG BEETLE
or Lunch with a MAGGOT?

Camilla de la Bédoyère and Mel Howells

Would you rather...

dine with a dung beetle,

drink with a mosquito,

have supper
with a spider,

or lunch with a maggot?

If you dined with a dung beetle, you'd have to eat a splendid dish of... elephant poo!

Dung beetles feast on elephant poo because it contains yummy stuff to eat which has passed right through the elephant's gut.

If you drank with a mosquito, you'd have to share a gloopy smoothie – made of blood!

Female mosquitoes need a blood meal before they can lay their eggs. It's full of goodness!

You'd have to join the spider for a feast of flies – not just for supper, but for every meal!

Spiders eat flies. They suck out their liquid insides, but leave the crunchy body bits!

Breakfast

Lunch

Supper

If you shared your packed lunch with a maggot, it'd be full of rotting flesh and scabs.

Maggots are baby flies and they mostly survive on a diet of dead and rotting animals – delicious!

Would you rather...

live with a snail,

a family
of termites,

a bookworm,

or a tick?

If you lived with a snail, you'd have to take your home with you wherever you go.

As you got bigger, your home would grow too, so it would always be the perfect size.

Termites are great builders so your home would be big and comfortable.

But this home would be made of mud mixed with termite spit and poo! You'd have to get used to it because one of these mud cities can last for 100 years!

You'd have to make your home in a good book because these tiny bugs find them a most delicious snack.

Bookworms sometimes go months without eating so once they find a book they like, they set up home and eat it from the inside out.

To live with a tick, you'd have to find a furry friend!

These beastly bugs have a disgusting habit of feeding on the animals they live on.

Would you rather...

have a queen bee
for a mum,

a water bug
for a dad,

a stick insect
for a brother,

or a millipede
for a sister?

A queen bee keeps a store of runny honey in her hive, so you wouldn't ever go hungry.

But she's got thousands of children that need feeding, so you'd have to join a long queue!

A water bug would give great piggybacks! He carries his baby eggs on his back until they are ready to hatch.

But you'd better watch out – he might take a bite if he fancies a snack! Hungry water bugs sometimes eat their own babies.

Don't play hide and seek
with your twiggy brother
because you'd never
be able to find him!

You might be able to smell
him though – some stick
insects make a foul stink
when they get scared!

If you had a
millipede as a sister,
you'd definitely
want her on your
football team!

A millipede
has up to 750 legs
so this bug would
be sure to score
lots of goals.

Would you rather...

dress like a caddisfly,

a caterpillar,

or an
orchid mantis?

It would be great to dress like a caddisfly, it's like wearing an invisible cloak!

Young caddisflies cover their bodies with anything they can find so they are excellent at blending into their watery surroundings.

Dressing like a caterpillar would mean covering yourself in bird poo!

When a swallowtail butterfly is still a caterpillar, it looks just like bird poo! This stops other creatures eating it for a tasty snack. Who wants to eat a lump of bird poo?

If you dressed like
an orchid mantis,
you'd blend in amongst
the pretty petals!

An orchid mantis looks
like a beautiful flower so it can
leap out and catch other insects
that it wants to eat.

Would you rather...

race like
a weevil,

be as strong as
a rhinoceros beetle,

cartwheel like
a flic-flac spider,

or high jump like
a froghopper?

You'd always pass the finishing line first if you had a neck like a weevil!

Giraffe-necked weevils have long necks to battle one another. They keep fighting until one gives up and runs away!

If you were as strong as a rhinoceros beetle, you'd be able to carry 10 elephants!

These beetles can carry 850 times their own weight. When they are in danger of being eaten by bigger animals, they use their great strength to dig deep into the ground to escape.

If you cartwheeled like a desert flic-flac spider,
you'd be able to do more than 25 in a row!

These spiders can move at about 2 metres per second to escape predators.

You could jump 100 times
your own height if you
were a froghopper!

Young froghoppers wrap
themselves up in a coat of
white spit-like froth to stop
birds from eating them. Adult
froghoppers simply leap out of
reach of a bird's beak!

Bug Awards!

Which bug would you rather be?

Mosquito

The Deadliest Bug

A mosquito spreads nasty diseases such as malaria and dengue fever, so this small bug kills more people than any other animal in the world.

The Bossiest Bug

A queen bee rules an entire kingdom of bees – as many as 60,000 bees can live in her hive!

Bee

Snail

The Slimiest Bug

A snail makes thick gloopy slime that protects its soft body as it slithers over rough surfaces, such as stones or prickly plants.

The Hungriest Bug

A caterpillar hatches from a tiny egg but it has to grow much bigger before it can turn into an adult butterfly or moth. It spends most of its time eating and it can double its size in just one day!

Caterpillar

Maggot

The Grossest Bug

Maggots breathe through their bottoms so they can keep breathing while they eat.

The Smartest Bug

A spider is super smart. Its brain is so big that it doesn't even fit in its head – it has to spread out into its legs! This big brain helps spiders build beautiful and complex webs.

Spider

More Bug Fun!

Stay safe and ask a grown-up to help you.

Bug watch

Hang a white sheet between two trees or on a washing line. When it is dark, shine a torch behind the sheet. Watch and wait while lots of flying insects fly to the sheet.

Would you rather...?

Think of some 'Would you rather...?' questions to share with your friends or family. Visit your local library and research different bugs to create your own fun questions.

Go pond dipping!

Half-fill a container with pond water. Use a small pond net, on a long cane, to scoop bugs out of the pond using a figure-of-eight movement. Place them in the container where you can watch them. Carefully return the bugs to their pond when you have finished.

Bug file

When you find a bug in the garden, park or pond, use a magnifying lens to look at it closely. Take photos or draw the bug so you can use books or the Internet to find out what type of bug it is. Make a note of where and when you found the bug, its colour and its size as well as any special features.

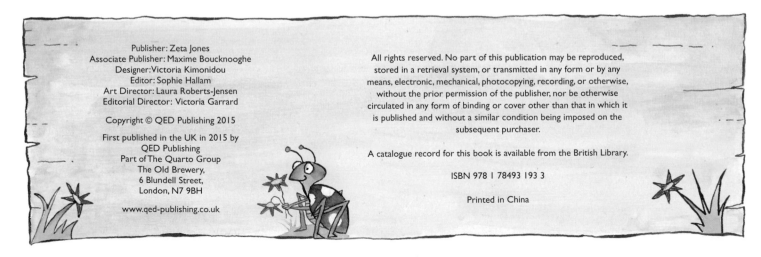

Publisher: Zeta Jones
Associate Publisher: Maxime Boucknooghe
Designer: Victoria Kimonidou
Editor: Sophie Hallam
Art Director: Laura Roberts-Jensen
Editorial Director: Victoria Garrard

Copyright © QED Publishing 2015

First published in the UK in 2015 by
QED Publishing
Part of The Quarto Group
The Old Brewery,
6 Blundell Street,
London, N7 9BH

www.qed-publishing.co.uk

A catalogue record for this book is available from the British Library.

ISBN 978 1 78493 193 3

Printed in China